Big Sh[ip]

A Rhyme for
Young Readers

by Richard Rensberry

Copyright © 2017, Richard Rensberry

All rights reserved.

No part of this publication may be reproduced, stored in a retrieval system or transmitted in any form or by any means electronic, mechanical, photo-copied, recorded or otherwise, without the prior written permission of the publisher and authors.

Published by: QuickTurtle Books LLC®

http://www.richardrensberry.com

ISBN: 978-1-940736-39-6
Published in the United States of America

If I were a big ship
I'd be the Sail-O-Set

anchored in the windswept
Bay of Marquette.

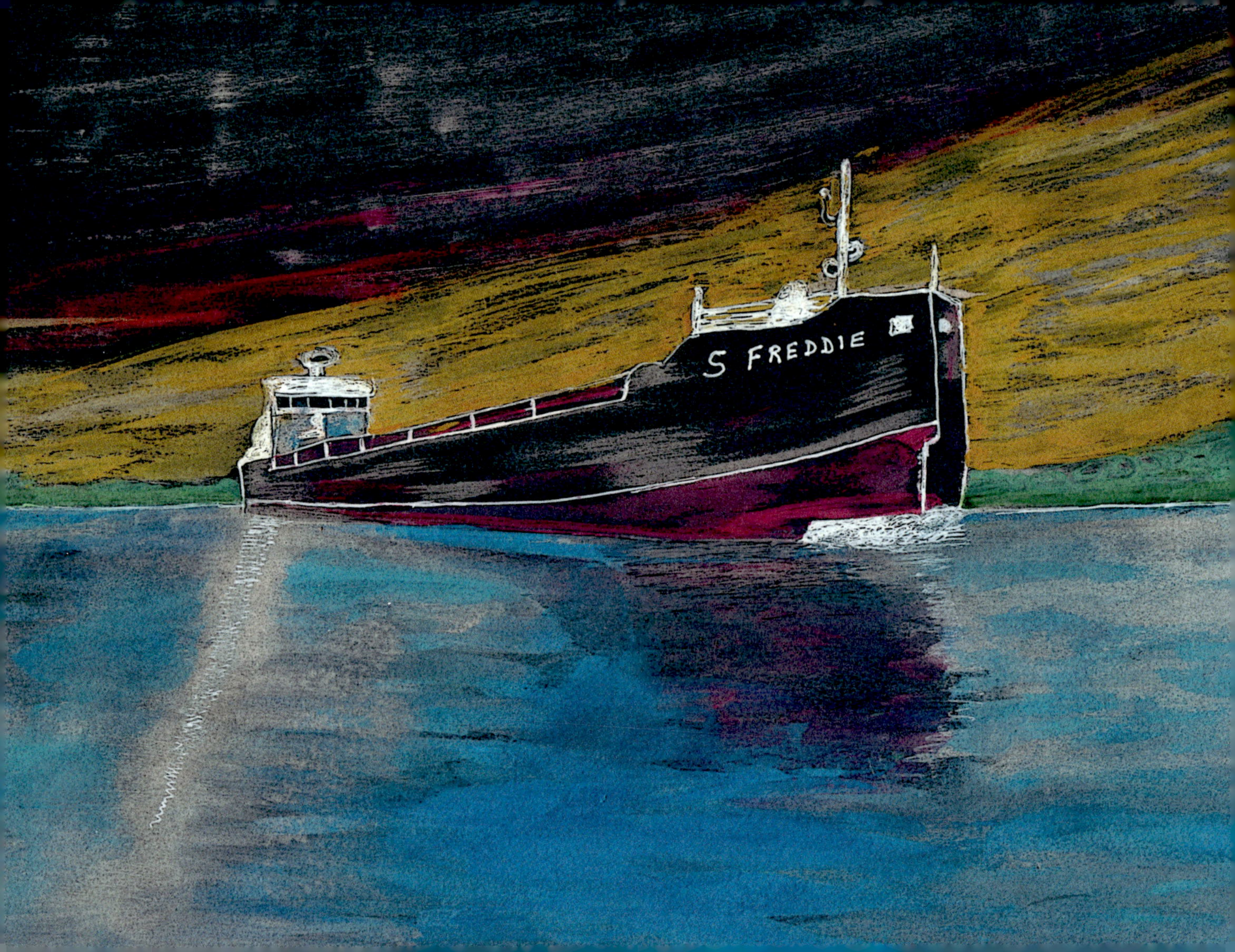
S FREDDIE

If I were a big ship
I'd be the S. Freddie
with lookouts in the wheelhouse,
binoculars ready.

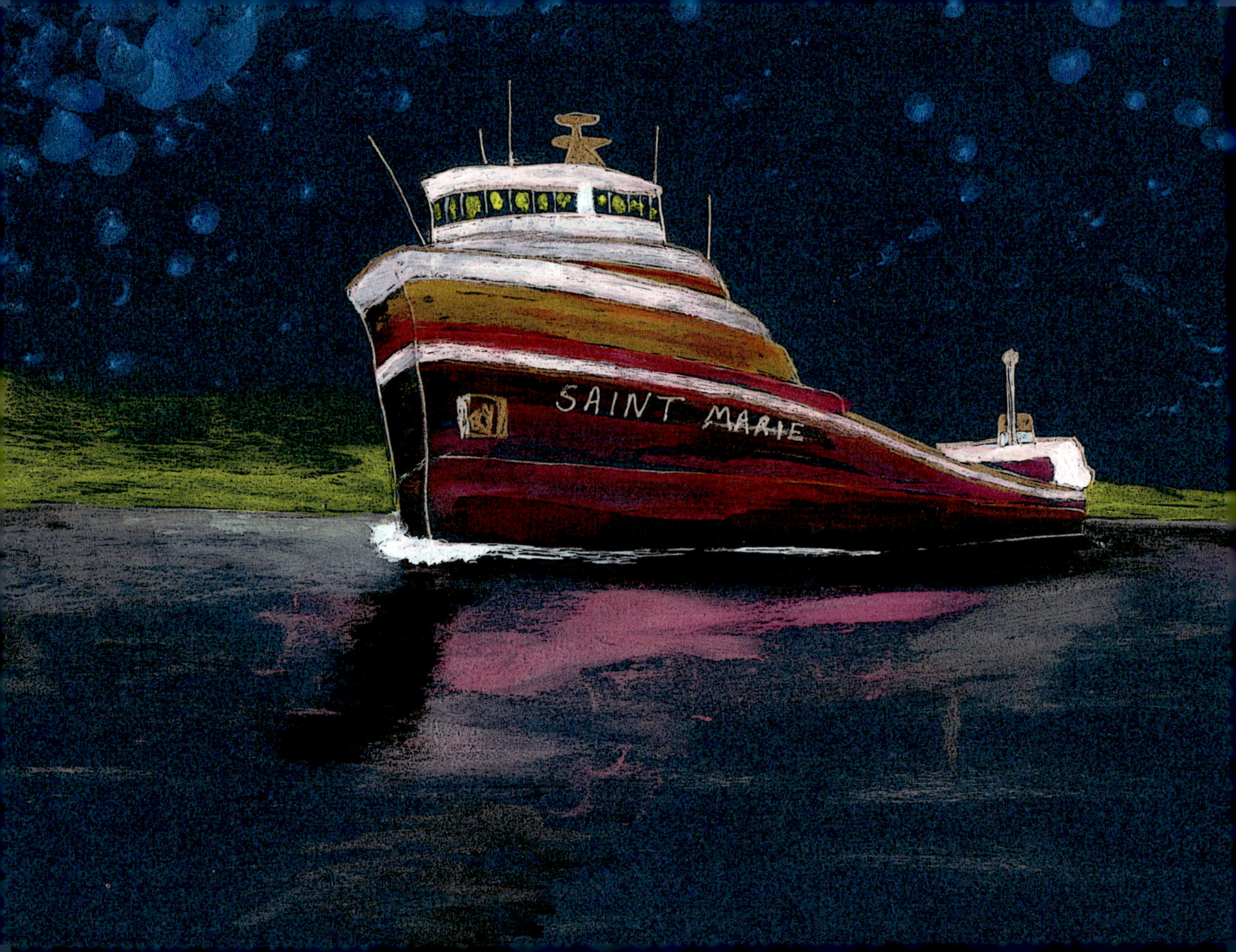
SAINT MARIE

If I were a Big Ship
I'd be the Saint Marie
with bulkheads full of iron,
lead and mercury.

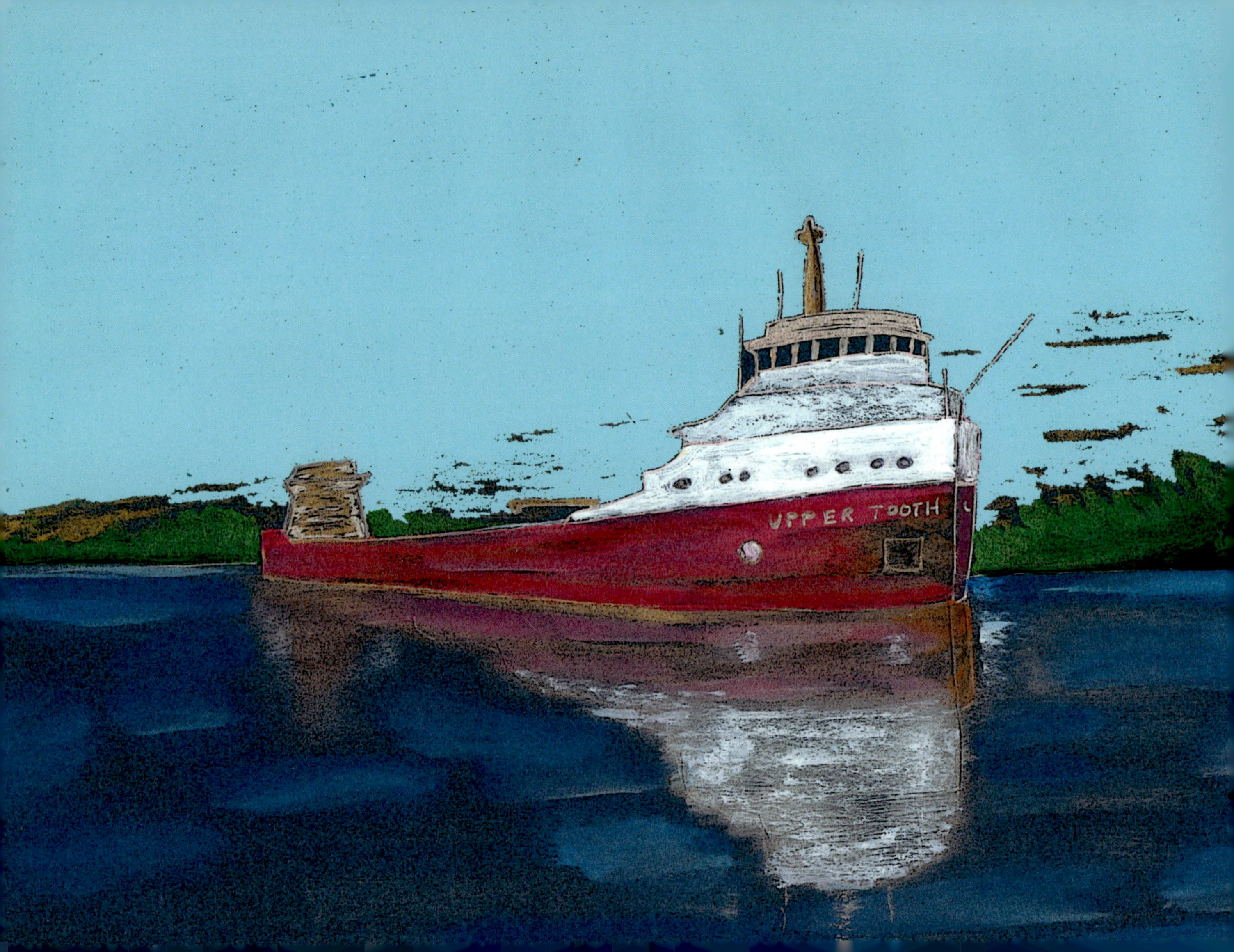
UPPER TOOTH

If I were a big ship
I'd be the Upper Tooth
water-lined by copper
and zinc from Duluth.

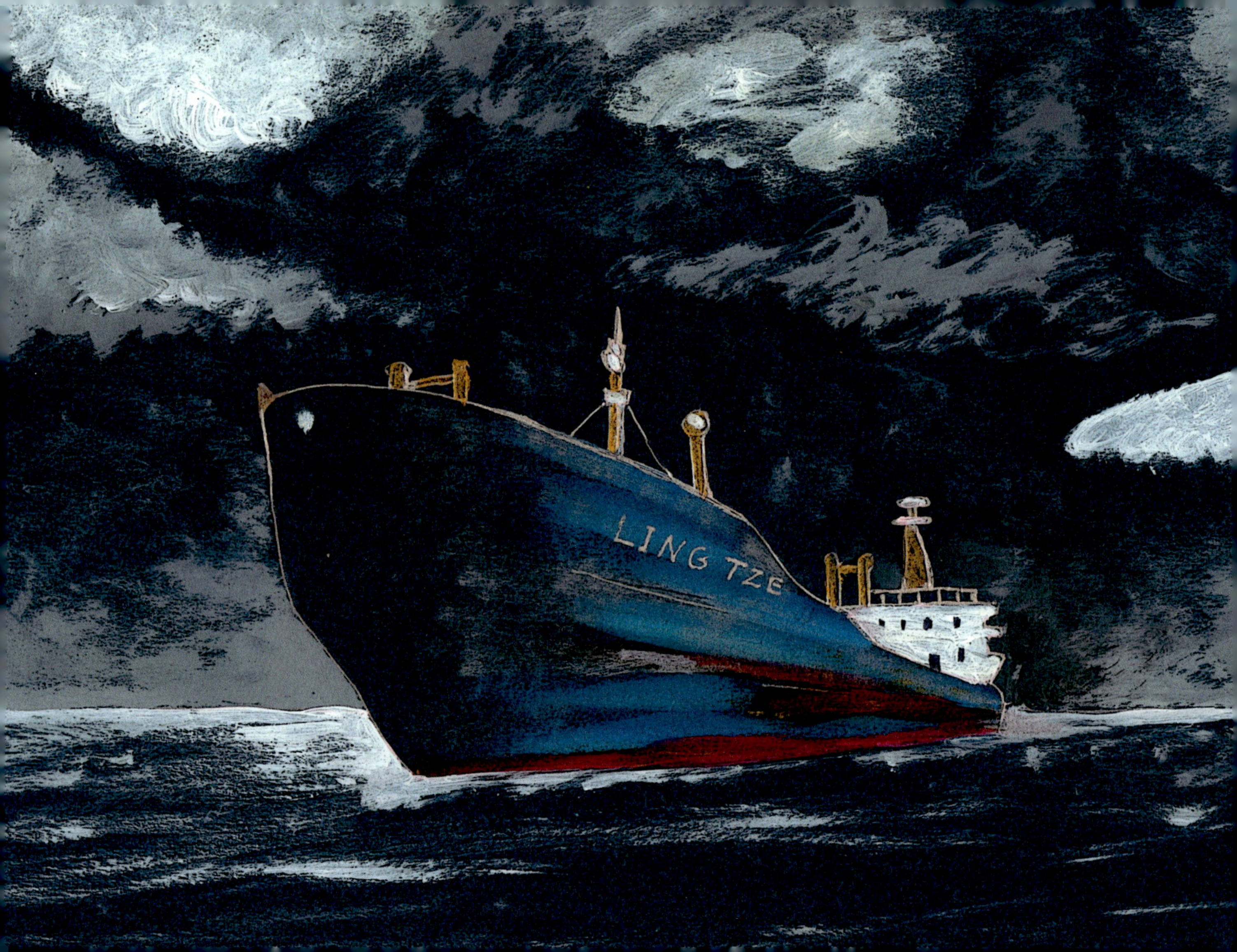
LING TZE

If I were a big ship
I'd be the Ling Tze
outbound from The Orient
across the China Sea.

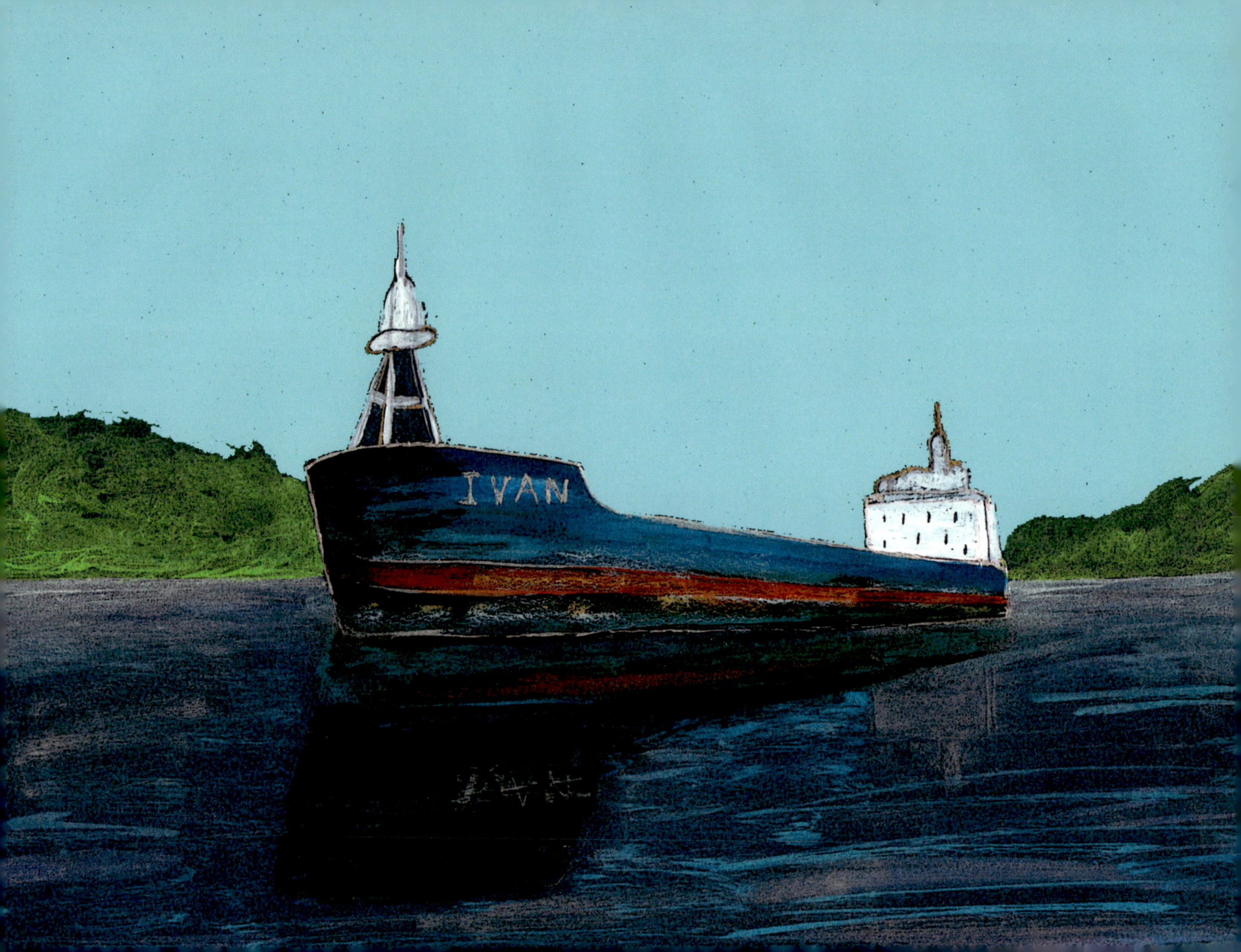
IVAN

If I were a big ship
I'd be the Ivan sent
all the way from Russia
for tons of dry cement.

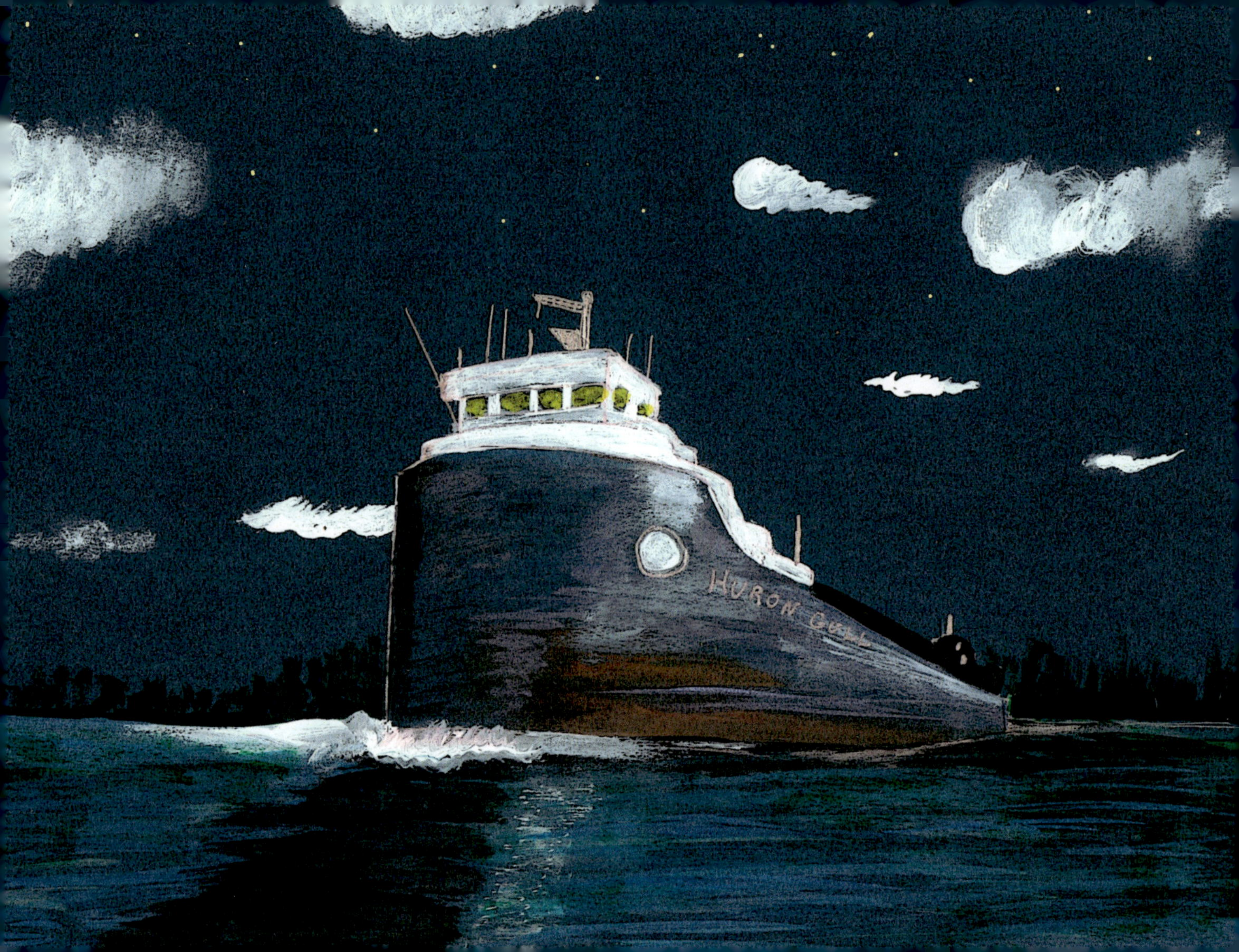

If I were a big ship
I'd be the Huron Gull
laden down with lumber
green upon my hull.

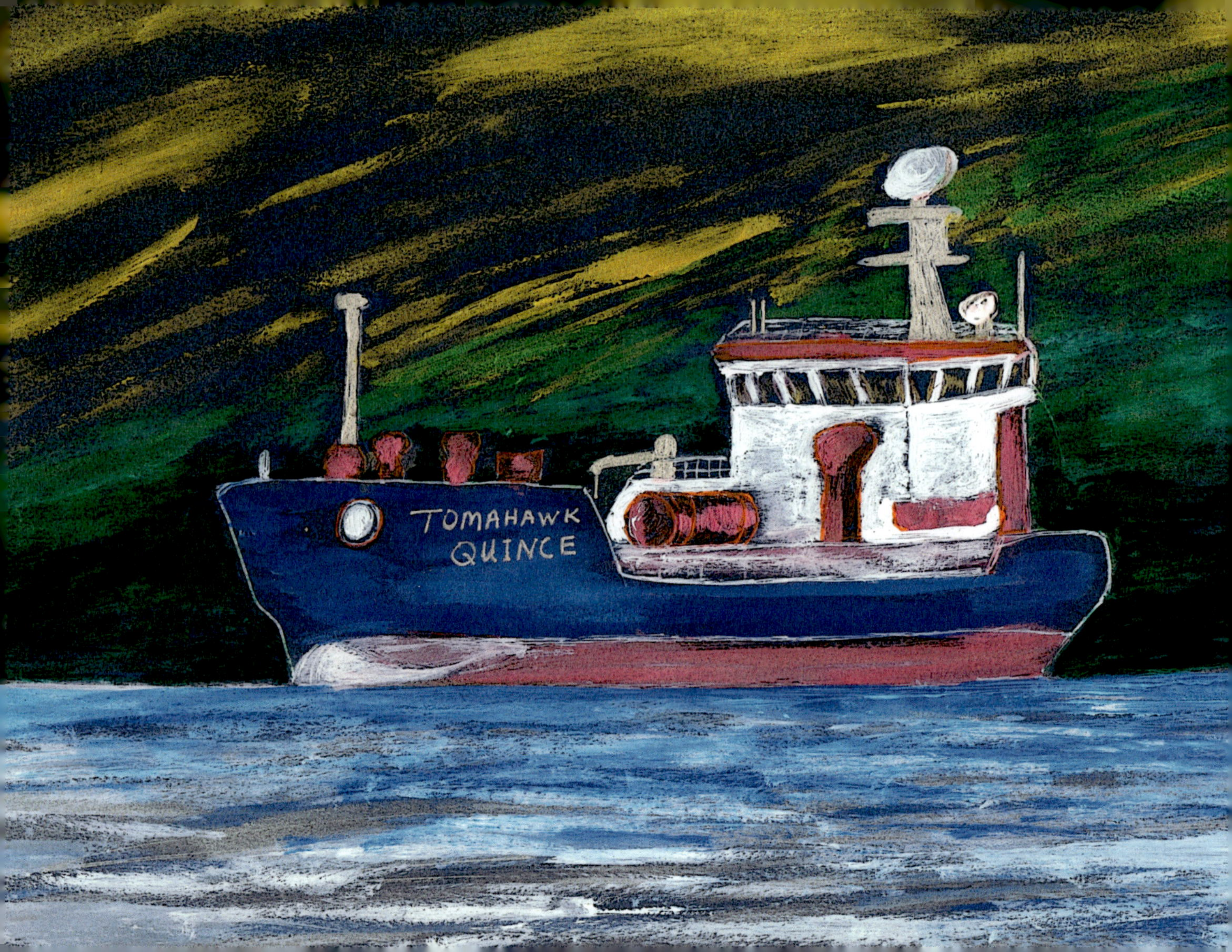
TOMAHAWK
QUINCE

If I were a big ship
I'd be the Port-A-Prince,
the Allegheny Queen
or the Tomahawk Quince.

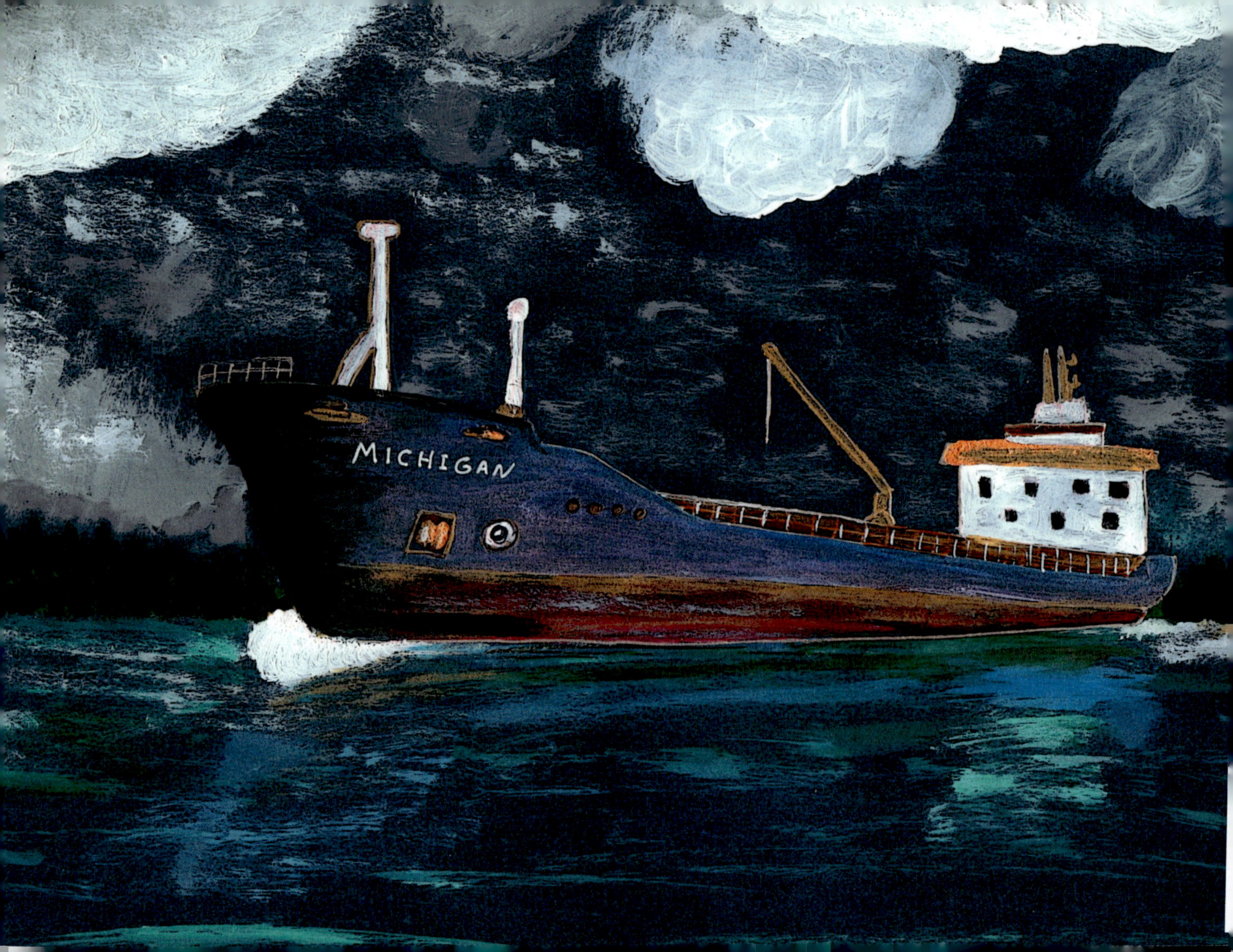
MICHIGAN

If I were a big ship
I'd be the Goodness Sakes
or maybe freighter Michigan
aboard the Greater Lakes.

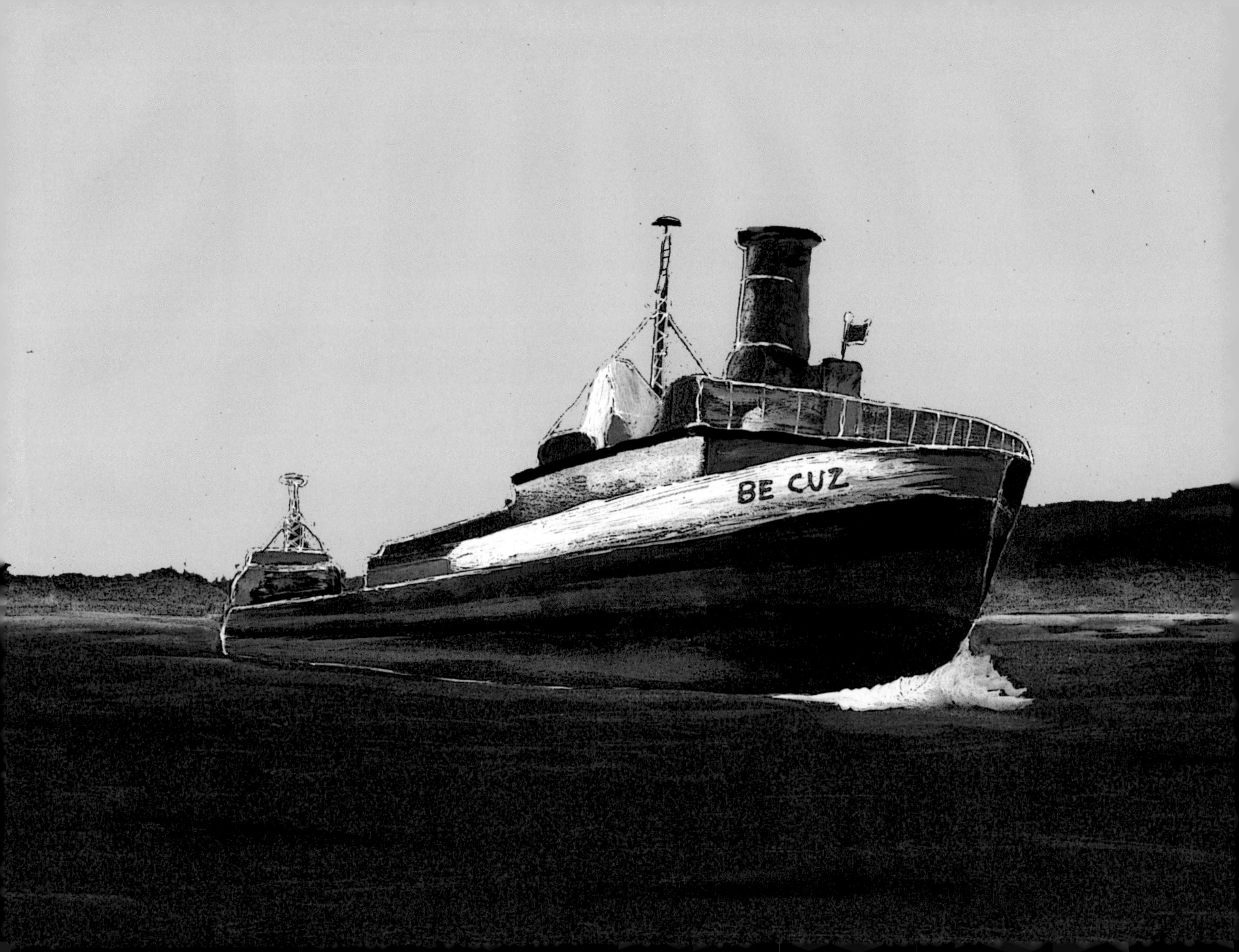
BE CUZ

If I were a big ship
I'd wonder how I was
christened Star of Heaven
or nebulous "Be Cuz".

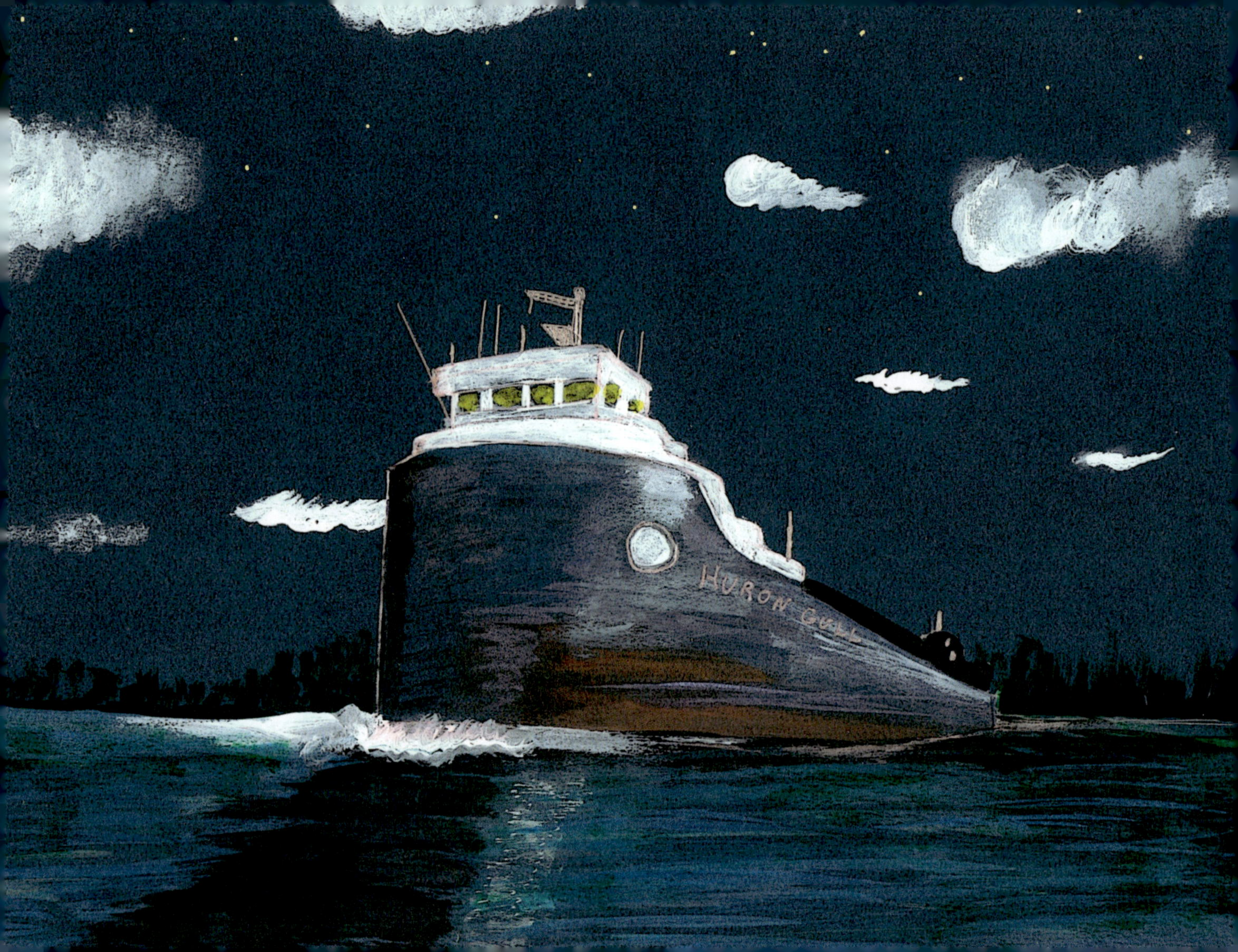
HURON GULL

The End.

More QuickTurtle Books in the Rhyme For Young Readers Series:

If I Were a Lighthouse
If I Were a Caterpillar
If I Were A Book
If I Were A Garden
If I Were A Heart
I Wish It Were Christmas
Goblin's Goop
Monster Monster
Colors Talk
Abigail's Chickens
The Blind Dove

Rhyme for Young Readers Glossary

1. windswept- battered by strong winds.
2. Marquette- City in the Upper Peninsula of Michigan located on Lake Superior.
3. wheelhouse- the command post of the ship from which the captain navigates.
4. bulkheads- walls or partitions separating the ship's compartments.
5. iron- ore for making iron and steel.
6. lead- industrial metal for many important products such as shields for radiation when you get x-rays at the dentist and doctor's office.
7. mercury- metal used in thermometers, lightbulbs and other products.

8. water-lined- a ship loaded to its maximum.
9. copper- metal used for plumbing and electricity.
10. zinc- industrial metal used to help other metals reach higher potential.
11. Duluth- City in Northern Minnesota located on the western most edge of Lake Superior.
12. outbound- in a direction away from.
13. The Orient- the far east area of the world, like China.
14. laden- loaded.
15. green- lumber that is freshly cut and not dried.
16. hull- main body of the ship.
17. christened- give a name to.
18. nebulous- not clearly understood or visible.

Made in the USA
Lexington, KY
15 April 2018